WHY NOT NOW?

WHY NOT NOW?

by
Mendek Rubin

Philosophical Library
New York

Published 1982 by Philosophical Library, Inc.
200 West 57 Street, New York, N. Y. 10019.
Copyright 1982 by Mendek Rubin. All rights reserved.
Library of Congress Catalog Card No. 80-84735.
SBN 8022-2380-X.
Manufactured in the United States of America.

Overseas distributor: George Prior Ltd.
52-54 High Holborn, London WC1V 6RL, England

This book is affectionately dedicated to my wife
Edith
and to my daughters
Ruth and Myra

CONTENTS

LIST OF ILLUSTRATIONS

xii

ACKNOWLEDGMENTS

I am indebted to Georganne W. Hendry for her editorial assistance; her encouragement helped to keep this project alive.

I wish to acknowledge the cooperation and enthusiasm of my wife, Edith, who shared with me the time of my struggle. She was most helpful throughout. It gives me pleasure to include some of her art works in this volume.

My thanks to Michael Margareten Cohen and to Mary Lee McIssac whose beautiful photographs are reproduced herein. Thanks also to Dianne Morse for the right to reproduce two of her works.

I should like to express appreciation to the following institutions who have graciously consented to the reproduction of some of their artwork:

The Art Institute of Chicago, Michigan Avenue at Adams Street, Chicago, Illinois 60603; Charles Scribner's Sons, 597 Fifth Avenue, New York, N.Y. (P. 32 from *Scribner's Magazine,* August, 1897, and p. 62 from *Scribner's Magazine,* December, 1898, reprinted by permission of Charles Scribner's Sons). The Detroit Institute of Arts, 5200 Woodward Avenue, Detroit, Michigan 48202; Fogg Art Museum, Harvard University, Cambridge, Mass. 02138; The Frick Collection, One East 70th Street,

New York, N.Y. 10021; The Metropolitan Museum of Art, Fifth Avenue & 82nd Street, New York, N.Y. 10028; The National Gallery of Art, Washington, D.C. 20565; New York Graphic Society, 140 Greenwich Avenue, Greenwich, Connecticut 06830; The Philadelphia Museum of Art, Benjamin Franklin Parkway, Box 7646, Philadelphia, Pennsylvania 19101.

M.R.

I ACCEPT THE BEAUTY OF REALITY.
THE SUN SHINES ON ME.

WHY NOT NOW?

Sometimes the clouds pass away and sunshine becomes
a reality.
Why not now?
Sometimes I am touched and my heart is filled with
gratitude.
Why not now?
Sometimes I know how rich and blessed I am.
Why not now?
Sometimes I am inspired and know that there is love.
Why not now?
Sometimes I feel that you and I are one.
Why not now?
Sometimes I know that freedom is my birthright.
Why not now?
Sometimes I care.
Why not now?

I WILL POSTPONE NO LONGER

I will postpone to be true to my feelings no longer.
    I need not wait till I am ready,
        I am ready now.
I will postpone using my strength no longer.
    I need not wait till I am ready,
        I am ready now.
I will postpone being my best no longer.
    I need not wait till I am ready,
        I am ready now.
I will postpone claiming my beauty no longer.
    I need not wait till I am ready,
        I am ready now.
I will postpone facing life no longer.
    I need not wait till I am ready,
        I am ready now.
I will postpone enjoying life no longer.
    I need not wait till I am ready,
        I am ready now.
I will postpone believing in love no longer.
    I need not wait till I am ready,
        I AM READY NOW!

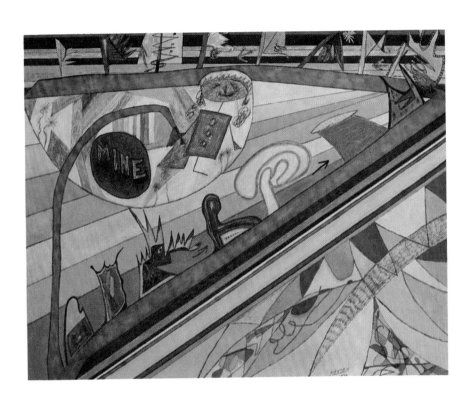

3

4

NIGHTMARE AT NOONTIME

I've been running, running all my life. I can't settle down. I can't enjoy the *now*. All my life I've been running on ahead. What am I running from? From myself? What am I running toward?

I see myself crossing a bridge. Now I find myself in a new
  landscape, full of light and joy, a place where people
  know me. They are shouting, "We love you—we love
  you."
But still I run.

I am slowing down now, tears running down my face. I
  can still hear the voices. "We love you—we love you."

I stop. Why was I running?
No need to run anymore.

THE WOES OF THE WANDERING MIND

Without direction, our minds wander.
Thought follows thought, undirected, uncontrolled,
    willy-nilly, helter-skelter.
Constantly we replay old hurts and pain. This is an
    addiction, and one that is deeply, profoundly
    destructive, for from our thoughts and the feelings
    they evoke flow the energy and actions of our
    personality.
Our thoughts should be our servants; they should
    constantly, effortlessly, add beauty and harmony to
    our lives.
When unwanted thoughts crowd in upon you, remove
    your mind from their vicinity by mentally visiting
Positive and life-enhancing situations.

7

8

THE GOLDEN LAKE

Visualize a warm, pleasant summer afternoon. You are surrounded by mountains and forests of pine. The quiet water and the beautiful surroundings give you a feeling of peace and serenity.

You have the magic power to turn the blue water into any color you wish. You visualize the lake turning the color of gold.

Slowly you enter the warm water of your golden lake. You feel the water's healing power flooding your body, mind, and soul.
Now you are shoulder-deep in golden water.

Let go! Surrender to the experience. You are in intimate contact with the color, with the water, and with the fresh green pines.

Stay in the water as long as you wish. Time does not matter here. When you are ready, you wade back to shore. Lie down on the fragrant grass. Let the sun warm and nourish you as you contentedly fall asleep.

10

TO THE HERE AND NOW

I sweep the floor,
I give it all my best.
I take a bath,
I give it all my best.
I clean my desk,
I give it all my best.
I do my job,
I give it all my best.
I walk in the street,
I give it all my best.
I meet a person,
I give him all my best.
I look at the sun and sky,
I give them all my best.
I see a raindrop,
I give it all my best.
To the most mundane,
I give all my best.
To the here and now,
To the here and now,
To whatever I meet in the here and now,
I give all my best.

WHAT AM I?

What am I
> but what I believe I am?

What am I
> but a mirror of what I perceive?

What am I
> but unfolding energy seeking its highest use?

What am I
> but a creation of infinite love?

What am I
> but a precious flower, a jewel communing with
> life?

What am I
> but a mystery wrapped in enchantment?

What am I
> but glory wrapped in spontaneous bliss?

What am I
> but a powerhouse of moss and steel?

What am I
> but an everlasting creator of infinite
> possibilities?

What am I
> but what I choose to be?

MY BOREDOM

My boredom covers
My fear of life . . ,
My boredom covers
My anger and rage . . ,
My boredom covers
My resignation and hopelessness . . ,
My boredom covers
My creativity and aliveness . . ,
My boredom covers
My sunshine and my joy. . .

15

16

VISUALIZATION: THE CLIMB

You are to climb a steep mountain.
You will need to use all your resources to reach the top.
You will have to use your will to succeed.
The climb is difficult—but you are determined.
To turn back is tempting, but you know you will be
*   rewarded for your effort.*
At the top of the mountain the real and the potential you
*   is waiting.*
This part of you is self-fulfilled, self-realized, full of joy.
Watch this joyful self run towards you as you continue to
*   climb.*
You reach the top, you reach your real self, you merge
*   with your higher self . . .*

You are now experiencing your real beauty.

It is peaceful, blissful, there on the mountain top.

18

ERROR, ILLUSION, AND COMPULSION

Error, Illusion, and Compulsion—
    How deeply I am caught in your web!
Error, Illusion, and Compulsion—
    How deeply and secretively you have managed to
    penetrate my being, emotions, and mind!
Error, Illusion, and Compulsion—
    You are not the real me!
    The real me still waits to be born.

20

THE GARDEN OF ROSES

You find yourself in the middle of a beautiful valley.
It is a delightful summer afternoon.
You are surrounded by a garden—it is known as "The
*   Garden of Roses."*
You are inspired by the beauty around you and your heart
*   is full of joy.*

A gentle breeze causes the flowers to rustle softly to and
*   fro.*
Each and every rose is sending forth its fragrance, its
*   beauty, into the Universe.*
The flowers bend in an exquisite dance, a celebration of
*   life.*
Suddenly you hear the flowers, the bushes, the grass, the
*   breeze,*
*   all calling your name.*
They whisper into your ears:
*   We love you.*
*   We accept you.*
*   We cherish you.*

COMPASSION

See the child in you and hold its hand.
Comfort this child. Say, "It's all right to be afraid,
everyone is, sometimes."

Tell the child that he or she is all right, no matter what.
Say, "I accept you as you are, all of you."

Hold the child close, and feel its pain.

Resolve to be more compassionate. Do it now.

Tell the child in you, "It's all right to be wrong
sometimes."
Tell the child in you, "I forgive you."
Tell the child in you, "I accept you and love you exactly
the way you are."

WHINING INSTEAD OF WINNING

My neighbors are not perfect. My children are not
 perfect.
My spouse is not perfect. My boss is not perfect. My job
 is not perfect. I am not perfect. The Government is
 not perfect. The weather is not perfect. Unions are
 not perfect.

Nothing is perfect . . .

Learn to recognize the complainer in you.
Take five deep breaths and relax. Allow the complainer to
 surface, with all your complaints.
In a detached way, allow your mature self to observe this
 whining and fretful child within. Take your time.
 Observe—do not pass judgment.

Realize that an attitude like this brings only pain.
 Realize that you are a victim of faulty thinking,
 and that by concentrating on what is lacking, you
 are prevented from enjoying the true wealth within
 your reach.

MEDITATION

To the killer within me . . .
   I confront you.

To the hopelessness within me . . .
   I light a candle to guide you.

To the victim within me . . .
   I raise you to your feet.

To the fear within me . . .
   I face you with courage.

To the cheat within me . . .
   I give you back good measure.

To the stinginess within me . . .
   I am generous with you.

To the cruelty within me . . .
   I soften your harshness.

To the distrust within me . . .
   I open to you in faith.

To the venom within me . . .
   I send you tenderness.

To the unforgivingness within me . . .
   I forgive you.

27

28

I HAVE A CHOICE

I have a choice—
>I can see the good in people or
>I can choose to dwell on their imperfections.

I have a choice—
>I can focus on the sunshine or
>I can choose to see only shadows.

I have a choice—
>I can see the glass as half-full or
>I can choose to see it as half-empty.

I have a choice—
>I can see that life wants to shower me with joy
and abundance or
>I can choose to pass life's treasures by.

I have a choice—
>I can deal with my rage and hatred or
>I can choose to project it onto others.

I have a choice—
>I can answer my soul's true needs or
>I can remain grubby and materialistically
demanding.

I have a choice—
>I can dare to be happy or
>I can choose to stay in the darkness.

I have a choice—
>What will I choose?

SOME SYMPTOMS AND THEIR CAUSE

A negative self-image is an obstacle to faith and to
success in all lines of endeavor; if we do not truly
believe that we deserve the best, we cannot truly
believe that good will come to us—and may reject it
when it does.

A negative self-image is hard to diagnose. So painful
are the feelings which it causes that often we push
them away from ourselves and onto others.
Statements such as these are the symptoms of a
negative self-image:
"Nobody loves me."
"It's all my parents' fault."
"Everyone is out for themselves."
"Life is meaningless."

Take a deep breath, quiet your mind, and relax.
Allow your own projections to surface. . . .
Whom do you blame for your misfortunes?
Observe the child in you. . . . see how he or she refuses to
take responsibility.

Don't judge . . . just observe.

Just being aware will bring change.

AN EYE EXERCISE

See yourself as a little child again.
Then visualize a wonderful person who takes care of
    you.
Look this person straight in the eye, the way a trusting
    child would do.
As you steadily look up into this kind face, you will feel
    loving rays beamed upon you.
You feel these rays nourishing you, warming you.
You feel your cares and troubles melting away.
You are at peace.

A DILEMMA

The child in us wants fun always.
The child can be destructive.
The child can be unreasonable.
The child can't take "no" for an answer.
The child believes everything belongs to him.
The child's energy is endless.
The child has no boundaries.

We create structures.
We create values.
We create boundaries.
We find the child in us is dangerous to our structures.
Then we try to squash the child.

Yet one without the other is only half a one;
The child in us needs the mature parent in us to tell him
    he is approved of and loved.
The child in us also needs the parent to discipline him.
And the parent, our mature self, needs the child, too.
The child has exuberance, vitality, spontaneity;
The child has the capacity to play.

Life is sometimes dull and we are machines
Unless we play.

RE-BORN

Imagine yourself being re-born . . .

This time, the choice is yours. Of course, you choose the most desirable place in the best country and the ideal parents. See your father in your mind's eye. Observe all his qualities: he is strong, self-assured, yet gentle and kind. He is also intelligent, witty, and resourceful. And you are the apple of his eye! The same is true of your mother.

Let your imagination go. See your new life pass before you: you are born—you are one year old—you take your first step—you say your first word—you go off for your first day of school—

You live in your dream house, surrounded by the people that you love best. You are nourished, physically and mentally. You are completely satisfied. All your needs are fulfilled.—

You are so happy! So happy!—

You develop into a young adult—you meet your first boy/ girl friend—

You are now a fully grown person, ready to accept responsibility for your life.

FEELING HOSTILE

Sometimes we are angry, especially when we can't
    control the situation.
Sometimes we harbor hostility against ourselves
    because we said or did something wrong. We make
    too many demands on ourselves and are
    embarrassed by our weaknesses and faults.
Sometimes we are like spoiled children—little dictators
    who run off in a huff when we can't have things our
    own way.

Write down all your angers and frustrations in a
    notebook. You can destroy the writings later if you
    wish.
Reason with the child in you and perhaps you can make
    him understand.
Realize that your faults and weaknesses and those of
    others which so enrage you, only prove that you are
    all human. You have made mistakes before. You
    will make mistakes again. What hurts you so much
    is not the errors. You are hurt by the feelings of
    rage which envelop you.

38

PATIENCE

If sometimes I am lonely,
    I will think of patience as strength.

If sometimes I am hopeless,
    I will think of patience as healing.

If sometimes I am frustrated,
    I will think of patience as love.

If sometimes I am unloveable,
    I will think of patience as virtue.

If sometimes I am poor,
    I will think of patience as the road to my inner
riches.

If sometimes I am aware of my imperfections,
    I will think of patience as leading me to the
gate of heaven.

If sometimes I am without faith,
    I will put trust in patience.

I will think of patience,
    I will think of patience,
        I will think of patience. . . .

BAD ACTORS

There's part of you that's weak and fearful and timid as
a rabbit, and part of you that has the courage of a
lion.
There's part of you which is stingy and Scrooge-like,
and a part that's generous to a fault. Each of us has
many aspects to our nature.

As children, because of our own particular situations in
life, we found it easier to get along by developing
certain parts of our personalities. We then
identified, often unconsciously, with these
developed aspects of our personalities and ignored
the other parts. We grew up believing that the well-
developed aspects were "all there was."

No wonder we feel weak and inadequate at times! We
are constantly meeting situations in life in which
more of our inner resources are needed—and these
resources have never been mobilized!

40

The next time you feel fearful or depressed, observe
    how that part of you which is weak and fearful
    takes over. This personality has center stage and
    won't give up the spotlight, even though its role in
    your life's drama has long ago been played.

The most effective way to deal with this bad actor is to
    turn the spotlight toward other, more positive
    aspects of your nature. If you persist and are
    patient, eventually these other traits of character,
    well-rehearsed, will step toward center stage to play
    their full parts.

WORRY: WHAT IT IS AND WHAT TO DO ABOUT IT

WORRY is a futile replacement for healthy concern.
WORRY is pessimism masquerading as positive action.
WORRY seeks trouble instead of the truth.
WORRY is the brain's bad habit, flourishing where
    faith is not.

Think back over your life.
How much time was spent worrying?
What good did it do?
How many of your imagined worries came true?

GOOD THINGS

Go back to your childhood, to a place you enjoyed a lot . . .
Think of a food you enjoyed a lot as a child . . .
Think of someone who was good and loving to you . . .
Think of a good deed you performed when you were
*   young . . .*
Think of a loving feeling you experienced toward
*   someone . . .*
Think of something you really like about yourself . . .
Think of something tender and sensitive about yourself . . .
Think of your potential as a human being . . .
Think of your struggles and your yearnings . . .

REACH FOR YOUR RICHES

We are as rich as the many things we are able to enjoy.
We are as poor as the many things we do not like.
For everything we reject,
We are left a little poorer.
For everything we learn to enjoy,
We become a little richer within.

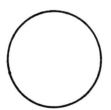

46

WHEN TO SAY NO

The tyrant of my lower nature wants to rule
    selfishly and cruelly
      —I say *no* to the tyrant.
The tyrant of my lower nature demands
    immediate gratification of every need.
      —I say *no* to the tyrant.
The tyrant of my lower nature accepts
    no rules save its own.
      —I say *no* to the tyrant.
The tyrant of my lower nature blames others,
    blames life for its pain.
      —I say *no* to the tyrant.
The tyrant of my lower nature whispers that love
    is weakness and will deplete.
      —I say *no* to the tyrant.
The tyrant of my lower nature projects hate
    onto others to hide its own.
      —I say *no* to the tyrant.
The tyrant of my lower nature ridicules
    divine law and universal justice.
      —I say *no* to the tyrant.
The tyrant of my lower nature seeks darkness
    and shuns light.
      —I say *no* to the tyrant.
The tyrant of my lower nature bullies me,
    cheats me, lies to me, confuses me.
      —I say *no* to the tyrant.

FORGIVE—AND LIVE!

To love others, we must first accept and love ourselves. For if we cannot accept and love this self of ours, this person we know the best, whom can we ever love? Sometimes, we find we cannot accept ourselves because we've said or done something "stupid," something which cannot be forgiven.

Here is a forgiveness exercise:

Stand erect, your feet planted on the floor, about a foot apart.
Pause. . . .
Feel your weight and become aware of your whole body.
Beginning with your feet, focus on each part of your body.
Become aware of your toes, your instep, your ankles.
Slowly move your focus of attention up your body until you reach the tip of your head.
Relax deeply . . . Pause . . .
Repeat to yourself, silently and slowly:
> *I forgive myself.*
> *I accept myself.*
> *I am alive.*
> *I am free.*

Repeat this statement. As you repeat it, it may sound as if one part of you speaks to the other part—that is all to the good.

I AM MOVING OUT

I let go of fear.
I want life.
> *I am moving out.*

I let go of hate.
I want love.
> *I am moving out.*

I let go of deprivation.
I want abundance.
> *I am moving out.*

I let go of separateness.
I want friendship.
> *I am moving out.*

I let go of bitterness.
I want happiness.
> *I am moving out.*

I let go of blindness.
I want wisdom.
> *I am moving out.*

I let go of doubt.
I want faith.
> *I am moving out.*

I let go of weakness.
I want strength.
> *I am moving out.*

I let go of limitation.
> *I am moving out.*
> I am moving out. . .

WHAT SILENCE HAS TO SAY

Find a comfortable spot, either sitting or lying down.
Relax your mind.
After a few minutes, begin to contemplate silence,
the silence of the ocean's depths,
the silence at the depth of the soul . . .

Allow yourself to surrender to this silence, and you are
deeply relaxed . . .

As you enter deeper and deeper into this silence,
you experience a sense of peace.
You realize that you do have options and choices in the
manner in which you choose to experience life . . .
You realize that you can change and improve on your old
ways of thinking . . .
feeling . . .
experiencing . . .
And then you also realize that you have outgrown your
old "friend," Anxiety.

HUMAN FAILINGS, HUMAN FEELINGS

To the part in me that is weak, insecure, vulnerable and
    scared,
And is too ashamed to admit it . . .

To the part in me that needs love and acceptance so
    badly,
And is too ashamed to admit it . . .

I say:

"Don't fight these feelings, for everyone has them.
Don't fight these feelings, for they are your humanity."

OTHER ASPECTS OF REALITY

Love is strength.
Creation is at my disposal.
Faith in myself can move mountains.
I can be open to love, I can take in people.
I can learn to be strong and effective.
I can learn to grow and change.
My inner strength is my greatest
                              treasure . . .

EXERCISE: FLASHBACK

Quiet your mind and relax deeply.

Now visualize your entire day. See yourself getting up in the morning and greeting your family.

How did you feel? Towards yourself? Towards your family?

Towards the world in general?

Visualize your working day, your encounters with others— co-workers, customers, shopkeepers.

Realize that you created this day, with your thoughts, feelings, and reactions to other people.

Are you pleased with this day?

Now re-create the day. If there was anger, or a sharp interchange with another, re-create this experience. Correct the anger with love and goodwill. If there was self-doubt or lack of confidence in any situation, re-experience that situation, visualizing yourself as strong, confident, and successful.

Realize that, just as you created this day, you will create tomorrow.

58

I AM YEARNING

I am yearning . . .
> I am yearning to be rid of selfishness
> and jealousy.

I am yearning . . .
> I am yearning to melt my hardness into
> gentleness and sweetness.

I am yearning . . .
> I am yearning for friendship that is free
> and unfettered.

I am yearning . . .
> I am yearning for compassion and
> acceptance for myself and all men.

I am yearning . . .
> I am yearning to express the glories of
> creation.

I am yearning . . .
> I am yearning for the peace that is mine
> and still eludes me.

I am yearning . . .
> I am yearning for the love I once knew
> and have forgotten.

I am yearning . . .
> I am yearning.

LIFE-GIVING LOVE

Beneath the veneer personality, in our real self, there is love for ourself and others.

This is an unshakable reality which we sometimes accept, but more often deny.

Much of our pain and alienation comes when we deny the reality of love.

Often, it takes an act of faith till this reality becomes apparent to us . . .

SAY GRR! TO THE "GORILLA"

The best way to understand anger is to turn it loose to
rip and roar.

EXERCISE:

Experience your anger.
Let yourself feel it.
You can kick (something soft) or shout or bang on
something (not your dog).
Become an observer and calmly watch yourself in this
state of rage . . .
Ask yourself—Why am I so angry?
Wait for the answer (some anger, felt now, may go back
to a half-forgotten yesterday).

Ask yourself—Who suffers from my anger?
Myself or the other person?

The alternative is to realize that anger is self-
destructive, and self-defeating. Resolve to rid
yourself of anger, and to keep a sense of humor in
all situations.

After all, you cannot smile and growl too. . . .

MORE ILLUSIONS

"I am a victim."
"It is weak to love."
"I cannot initiate loving relationships."
"Others must love and approve of me at all times."
"I must prove my worth again and again."
"I cannot be happy unless I am perfect."
"I should never be sad or depressed."
"Only Money gives security."
"Stubbornness is strength."

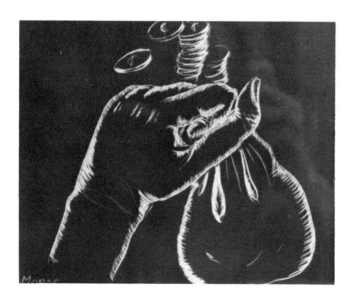

EXERCISE: YOUR MENTAL INVENTORY

*A. Think of everything you like about yourself and your
       life;*
Good qualities
Your successes
Anything about your life that makes you feel good.

B. Think of everything that is wrong with your life;
Your inadequacies
Your worries
Your dislikes.

C. Go through these two lists in you mind.
Which is longer, A or B?
*Estimate the amount of thought you give daily to items on
       list A.*
How much time on list B?
Take your time.

D. Ask yourself what meaning this has for you.
*E. Now think of all the people you know whose plight is
       worse than your own. . . Compare your problems with
       theirs . . .*
F. Ask yourself what meaning this has for you. . . .

ANXIETY

Anxiety whirs in the air around us, seeking a nest in
which to hatch worry and woe.
Anxiety is catching and spreads like a germ.
Sometimes we sense, in particular surroundings,
someone's anxiety hovering around. "Bad vibes"
we say.
As you grow more perceptive, you will learn to
recognize anxiety and laugh in its face. But even
though a part of us doesn't like it, sometimes we
welcome it, because we know it so well.
For all our lives we have been conditioned to live with
anxiety and fear.

Ask yourself: "Do I really want to give it up?"

EXERCISE: FOCUSING

The purpose of this exercise is to learn to focus and
    control the mind.

Find a quiet place where you will not be disturbed.
Allow yourself five to ten minutes for this exercise.

*Turn your head slowly from side to side, using four of the
    five senses—sound, sight, touch and smell—to become
    intensely aware of your surroundings.*
*Try to encounter your surroundings as if you were seeing
    them for the first time.*
Whenever your attention lessens, come back . . .

Strive for a heightened sense of feeling "at one" with
yourself and with your surroundings . . .

68

SELF INDULGENCE-SELF AFFLICTION

My self-indulgence decrees:
"Perfection every day"
And this trying to be what I am not becomes very tiring.

My self-indulgence issues forth a stream of
new needs, new wants daily;
With the result that I am never satisfied—
My needs can never be fulfilled.

My self-indulgence belches forth
blame and anger
Polluting the atmosphere
Causing pain to me and hurting others.

And then—my self-indulgence wails:
"Poor me! Alas, poor me!"

FEELING HOPELESS

When there are clouds, say:
    I WANT LIGHT, I WANT LIFE, I WANT LOVE.
When darkness surrounds you, say:
    TOMORROW WILL BRING LIGHT.
When things look blackest, say:
    I WILL FIGHT THROUGH THE DARK DAYS,
                UNTIL I REACH:
          LIFE

          LIGHT

          LOVE.

Remember that nothing is ever hopeless.

VISUALIZATION: A BASKET OF FLOWERS

Relax deeply. . . .
Visualize yourself holding a basket of flowers, your
    favorite ones.
Visualize people, all kinds of people, young, old, some you
    like, some you don't like.
See them approach you, one by one.
Each tells you "I love you."
You respond by saying: "I accept your love," and give
    each person a flower.
Do this until the basket is empty . . .

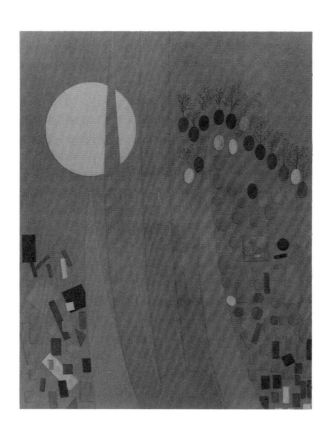

74

AT PEACE

I am as calm as the *sunrise*
    because there is a *new day* dawning.

I am as calm as the mystery of a golden *sunset*
    because of the *fascination* within me.

I am as calm as the *rose*
    because I know my *beauty*.

I am as calm as the *stallion*
    because I have *poise*.

I am as calm as the music of the *spheres*
    because of the harmony *within me*.

I am as calm as the *snowflake*
    because I melt with my *feelings*.

I am as calm as the *sea*
    because I am *immortal*.

I am as calm as *all*
I am as calm as *all*.
    Because I am at peace.

THE CHAINED TIGER

My passivity
        is anger and hate.
My passivity
        is the withholder of my vital energies.
My passivity
        is a ship eternally anchored.
My passivity
        is the blamer and the accuser.
My passivity
        is the intention never to open and love.
My passivity
        is secret rebellion against God.
My passivity
        is still water needing to flow.
My passivity
        is a child needing to grow.
My passivity
        is snarled energy needing to unfold.

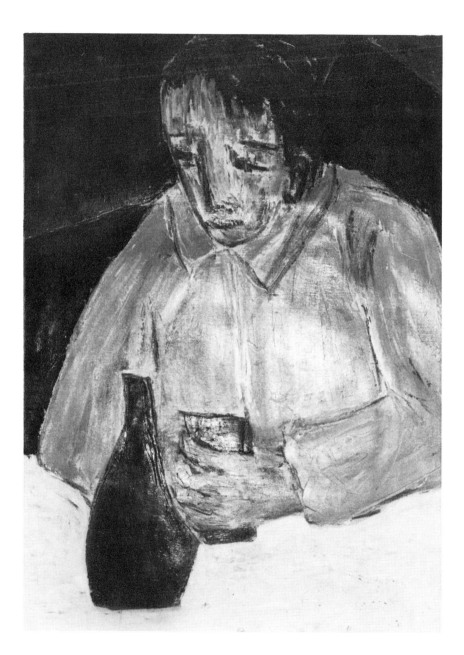

78

LIGHT A CANDLE

See your problems basically as symptoms of being in
darkness.

Light a candle . . .

Equate the light from the candle, with the GREATER
INTELLIGENCE.

*As you stare at the flame, allow the illumination to en-
lighten you.*
*Allow the GREATER MIND to do work for you, so that
you may get new insight to your problems.*

The answer will come . . .
     tomorrow, next month, next year . . .
        It will come. . . .

FEAR

Someone once said, "Fear is faith in the wrong outcome."

Examine your fears in light of this statement.
Now take five deep breaths and relax.
Be calm and become the observer. Tell yourself, "I have
    fear, but I am not my fears."
Take as much time as you need and let your fears surface.
What are your fears.
Fear of failure?
    Fear of failure is lack of faith in yourself.
Fear of people?
    To fear people is to lack faith in yourself and others.
Fear of life?
    To fear life is to reject its beauty.
Fear of illness and disaster?
    To fear that the worst will happen is to lack faith
    that the best can happen.
Again take five deep breaths and relax.

Learn from your fear by considering its nature. Consider,
and affirm:
> FEAR CAN TEACH ME COURAGE,
> WHOSE OPPOSITE IT IS.
> FEAR CAN TEACH ME COMPASSION,
> FOR EVERYONE FEARS.
> FEAR CAN BE A BLESSING BECAUSE
> FEAR CAN TEACH ME FAITH . . .

VISUALIZATION: THE DIALOGUE

You are facing a mirror. You are having a dialogue with yourself.

Q: Have I been good to you lately?
wait for the answer.

Q: Have I been your best friend and defense attorney?
wait for the answer.

Q: Do I demand too much from you?
wait for the answer.

Q: How can I appreciate you more?
How can I become a better friend?

Wait for the answer.

82

FEELING "ALL ALONE"

Why do I feel alone?
Why do I feel hopeless?

I need to reach out
But I don't know how . . .

I close my eyes
I listen to the depth of my pain and despair.
There, in the dark depth of my pain,
I see a little child reaching out its hand to me.
I embrace the child, I calm it.
I nourish it, I encourage it, I love it.
I reach out to this child in me.
Thus I learn to reach out to all others.
Then I'm no longer alone.

FEELING HURT

Have a dialogue with the child in you.
  "Why are you hurt?"
  (Be patient, let the child answer.)
  Is there anything else that bothers you?"
  (Stay with the child for five minutes or so. Let the hurt come out in the open.)

Tell the child:
  "I want to help you. I feel your pain and know how vulnerable you are. What would you like me to do?"

Now get in touch with your real self, the self that is strong, good, loving, and free. Ask it for help. Ask it to expand your capacity for forgiving. Ask it to expand your capacity to love.

Let the hurt wash away. Put on your beautiful garment and enter the place of meditation in your mind.

85

EXCESS BAGGAGE

Quiet your busy mind and relax deeply. Become aware of all your negative attachments and of how they control your life. You know so much pain, loneliness, and unhappiness— all because you are not being yourself.

Imagine yourself setting out for a long journey, weighed down with all sorts of bundles, back packs, knapsacks. Just so has your free spirit been weighed down with fear, doubt, and the woes of the world around you.

See yourself travelling with all these bundles, and see yourself become very tired and unable to bear the weight anymore. Let go of the strings of habit which tie these burdens to you. You are shedding all that is false and unreal, all self-defeating habits.

Think of the areas where you doubt yourself, God, life, people—shed these self-doubts.

Feel, for a while, the discomfort and insecurity of your new state—it's a strange, light, almost naked feeling. Feel new strength and power surging through you. Now walk away— light, free, and strong—out into life.

ONLY BY LOVING

Only by loving life
      can I live.
Only by loving love
      can I love.
Only by loving my friends
      can I deserve them.
Only by loving abundance
      can I have abundance.
Only by loving beauty
      can I have beauty.
Only by loving truth
      can I attain it.
Only by loving creation
      can I create.
Only by loving myself
      can I love others.
Only by loving life
      can I live.

HUMILITY

I don't know—
Why am I the way I am?

I don't know—
What makes me want the things I want?

I don't know—
Why do certain things make me happy?

I don't know—
Why is there love, why is there hate?

I don't know—
Why is there life, why is there death?

I don't know—
What is really good for me or anyone else?

I don't know—
Perhaps I don't even know that
                    I don't know. . . .

90

ULTIMATE REALITY

In the final analysis, I have only myself.
In the beginning, in between and at the end . . .

My career, family, education, country, race, etc.
When it comes down to it, should be considered the
    frosting on the cake only . . .

Yet it is a gift to be alive . . .

LIVING OFF THE TOP AND LIVING IN THE NOW

To be happy means to live fully and to feel and experience life deeply. It means doing away with boredom, dead time, and apathy. It means having our attention engaged and all our senses in use each moment, as we more fully explore the world and its changing wonders.

EXERCISE: AWARENESS

Try to visualize, as vividly as possible, an occasion when you experienced visual pleasure.

Recall the different aspects of the experience—physical, mental and emotional.

PAUSE

Now imagine yourself in an expanded state of awareness:
Happy with life, happy with yourself.
Try to visualize again the same experience.

Remember to act as an impartial observer,
You can repeat the exercise with other senses:
Listening   tasting   touching.

The goal is to live in an expanded state of awareness—now and forever! You can see that the happier we are, the more awareness we have. Then the grass is greener, the rose smells sweeter, etc., etc. And the more aware we are, the more happiness we have.

I NEED YOU NO MORE!

Anger—   You kept me down for years.
                  I need you no more.

Hate—   You kept me down for years.
                  I need you no more.

Pride—   You kept me down for years.
                  I need you no more.

Laziness—   You kept me down for years.
                  I need you no more.

Dependency—   You kept me down for years.
                  I need you no more.

Despondency—   You kept me down for years.
                  I need you no more.

*Self-deprivation—*You kept me down for years.
                  I need you no more.

Fear—   You kept me down for years.
                  I need you no more.

WHAT DO I THINK?

Heaven and hell are on earth, in our thoughts, our beliefs, and in the feelings born of those thoughts and beliefs.

It is not what we *have* that makes us happy or unhappy—It is what we *think* we have that makes the difference.

It is not what we *are* that makes us happy or unhappy—It is what we *think* we are that makes the difference.

THE POWER OF OUR BELIEFS

If you think that some of these beliefs apply to you:
> "I am deserving"
> "I am a winner"
> "I am a good person"
> "I am lovable"

The result will be: HAPPINESS

If you think that some of these beliefs apply to you:

> "I am a loser"
> "I am unlovable"
> "I am so poor"
> "I am hopeless"

The result will be WORRY, FEAR, DESPAIR.

□

98

THE HAPPY THOUGHT ROLL CALL

This is an exercise to help de-magnetize negative thought patterns by substituting life-giving thought patterns in their stead.

1. Make a list of recent instances when you felt success-ful, triumphant, proud of an accomplishment, or par-ticularly happy.

2. Now go back over your life and expand the list. In-clude small joys as well as momentous ones.

3. Read the list daily. Try to memorize it.

4. Make a habit of reviewing the list just before you fall asleep and again upon waking.

This list will become a great treasure in your life. The list can come out, the roll call can be made, whenever you have a difficult moment in your day.

GOD TO CHILD

God: What is your pain my child?
Child: I know not of any.

God: What is your pain my child?
Child: Who are you anyway that you want to know?

God: What is your pain my child?
Child: I'd rather hear you not.

God: What is your pain my child?
Child: You mean nothing to me. Convince me of
your existence!

God: What is your pain my child?
Child: I am so busy. You're intruding.

God: What is your pain my child?
Child: Playing my favorite game, hating my brothers
and sisters.

God: What is your pain my child?
Child: I can't take the sunshine. I can't see the light!

God: What is your pain my child?
Child: That you love me, but . . .
                          That I won't take it in. . . .

JUST ORDINARY

After pondering the fact that I am ordinary.
       I bury my face in a rose.

After imagining a golden sunset.
       I see myself just ordinary.

After pondering the fact that I am ordinary.
       I sing "Pagliacci" in the shower.

After imagining a butterfly's wings.
       I see myself just ordinary.

After pondering the fact that I am ordinary.
       I embrace an old friend with a heart full of
       love.

After imagining a seashore stretching to infinity.
       I see myself just ordinary.

After pondering the fact that I am ordinary.
       I swim in the ocean like a skillful fish.

After imagining a distant mountain. . . .
       I see myself just ordinary.

After experiencing God as love . . .
       I see. myself just ordinary. . . .

104

WHERE TO GO FOR HELP

Sit or lie down.
Breathe deeply——relax deeply.
Give your complete attention to your toes, your feet.
Feel the blood flowing down to them, they may feel slightly heavy.
When you feel your feet are relaxed, confirm it by saying,
> *"My feet are relaxed."*

Then go up your body, every part of it, applying the same method. When you have relaxed body and mind, make the affirmation:
> *"My body is relaxed. My mind is relaxed."*

Repeat this affirmation a few times.

Now visualize yourself walking up a mountain path. You are feeling expectant and excited because you know that on the mountain top something important awaits you.

Now you reach the top. Look around at the breathtaking view. Breathe in clean healing air.——Sit down and close your eyes——A few feet away from you, a special person will appear. This person may be someone you know well, or someone you see for the first time.

Go to this person and tell him or her your troubles and anxieties . . . Speak as freely as you can, this person is very loving and understanding. When you are finished ask for advice . . . ask what you have to do at this point in your life.

If the answer doesn't come right away, be patient and ask again, confidently expecting an answer.
Finally, thank your Guide for help.

THE GODS ARE CRYING

When one stops running and the mind
becomes silent,

When one is relaxed and listens to the stillness
of the void

One hears the Gods crying . . .

They are wondering where they went wrong
with mankind:

Was giving them a free choice really such a
good idea?

They wanted us to be free,
They wanted us to be strong,
They wanted us to use reason,
They wanted us to respect each other,
They wanted us to care. . . . . . .

108

WILD ANIMALS IN THE HOME AND WHAT TO DO ABOUT THEM

Certain unpleasant aspects of ourselves—
Fear, anger, greed,
Envy, cruelty, and self destructiveness—
Can be compared to jungle animals.
Some are dangerous,
Some sting and are poisonous—
And somehow or other we let them into the house.

Now they are part of us—
But the wonderful thing is:
When we recognize them,
When we face up to them—
They change.
Slowly they become tame, tolerable—
Even beautiful.
Then we have nothing to hide—
Our house is open to all.

110

MOURNING

When we lose a loved one, a parent, a child, a friend,
We must go through a period of mourning. We need to
feel and experience the pain and loss of the
separation, in order to be able to function as a
healthy individual.

WE ARE ALL ONE

The child and the adult in us, our minds, bodies,
feelings, should all work in harmony and
support each other. They are our inner family.

When any part of us is disconnected, separated or un-
acknowledged, the results are alienation of the self and
pain . . .

We need to know it, and ponder its meaning and understand how it affects everything in our life.
Then admit the feelings of loss and mourning.
Often after going through a period of mourning, a new
blossoming, like a spring flower, will shine forth its ra-
diance and we will find a new lease on life. . . .

112

BY MYSELF

I alone
      can light my life's candle.
No one will
      No one can
            No one should
                  Light it for me.

I alone
      can direct my mind's force.
No one will
      No one can
            No one should
                  Direct my life for me.

114

AWARENESS

The number of stimuli which awareness permits our consciousness to experience is a measure of our being alive.

Our happiness depends to large degree on the extent of our awareness of life, people, a flower, the sky; of the different surfaces we touch, the scents we smell and the sounds we hear; of the variety of color around us.

To the extent that we open our inner door to the world's stimuli, and to the extent that we are aware of our own feelings, thoughts and beliefs; of the variety of choices open to us . . .

To this same extent the more truly alive we are and the more together we feel . . .

And the happier we can become.

ON LEARNING

When I learn to enjoy another's happiness
  I am happier myself.

When I can perceive another's beauty
  I get in touch with my own.

When I can appreciate another's wisdom
  I add to my store of knowledge.

When I learn to submit to a greater authority
  I learn to develop my own.

IN THE MIDST OF THE STORM

In the midst of my despondency and turmoil
      Yet I know
suffering and sorrow can be nature's tool to show us our
      souls' dark corners and help our minds bear
      fruit

In the midst of my despondency and turmoil
      Yet I know
after the storm there is calm and after the darkness comes
      light.

120

MY TRUE NEEDS

I need to know that I am free
      so I can feel my strength.

I need to know that I am free
      so I can allow others to be what they are.

I need to know that I am free
      so I gain back my dignity.

I need to know that I am free
      so I know why life is worth living.

I need to know that I am free
      so I give myself the freedom to be.

122

THE BACKWARD CHILD

Even though I don't care
I am still a child of the universe;
The sun shines down
And nature still sustains me.

Even though I don't care
Someone still finds me deserving
And saves me a seat at the banquet
Where the lovers of life are feasting.

Even though I don't care . . .

124

STOP AND LISTEN

Sometimes in the midst of my worrying and my rushing
        And my pursuit of power and fame,
Sometimes while keenly concentrating
        On what is wrong with the world, and with me
I hear a voice within me
Loudly entreating,
        "Listen . . . Listen . . . Listen . . .
        I am here, in this moment . . .
        Stay with me now.
        Life is here in this very moment
        Live it now and live it well."

I AM GRATEFUL

If I had only one blissful moment in my life
      I am grateful . . .
If I felt love but once
      I am grateful . . .
If I perceived beauty but once
      I am grateful . . .
If I perceived myself immortal but once
      I am grateful . . .

128

I SEE A TREE GROWING

Growing taller and taller, getting stronger and stronger.
Spreading out and reaching out to the world, to the sky,

SO DO I . . .

Life, nature or God desires the tree to blossom,

SO DO I . . .

ALL IS ONE

I am all . . .
> I am the mountain,
> I am the valley,
> > I am all . . .

I am all . . .
> I am the summer,
> I am the fall,
> > *I am all . . .*

I am all . . .
> I am the heaven,
> I am the earth,
> > *I am all . . .*

I am all . . .
> I am the sunrise,
> I am the sunset,
> > *I am all . . .*

I am all . . .
> I am the laughter,
> I am the pain,
> > *I am all*

I am all . . .
> I am all visions,
> I am all that knows
> > *I am all . . .*

I AM ALL, I AM YOU, YOU ARE ME, WE ARE ALL. . . .

THERE IS MUSIC WITHIN ME

There is music within me.
            I want to hear it.
There are colors within me.
            I want to see them.
There is knowledge within me.
            I want to claim it.
There are riches within me.
            I want to enjoy them.
There is creativity within me.
            I want to use it.
There are tastes within me.
            I want to savor them.
There is laughter within me.
            I want to open to it.
There are mysteries within me.
            I want to pursue them.
There is greatness within me.
            I want to live it.
There is God within me.
            I NEED WANT NO MORE. . . .

134

I SEE A PERSON

I see a person lying in a beautiful meadow,
    So happy.
        It is I.
I see a person very loving, very giving,
    So happy.
        It is I.
I see a person laughing with friends,
    So happy.
        It is I.
I see a person mature and responsible,
    So happy.
        It is I.
I see a person singing in the shower,
    So happy.
        It is I.
I see a person strong and courageous,
    So happy.
        It is I.
I see a person living in harmony,
    So happy.
        It is I.
I see a person self-realized, God-like,
    So happy.
        It is I.